in her own words

Cher

Nigel Goodall

OMNIBUS PRESS

Copyright (c) 1992 Omnibus Press
(A Division of Book Sales Limited)

Edited by Chris Charlesworth
Cover & book designed by 4i Limited
Picture research by David Brolan

Special thanks to Vivienne Singer for her
invaluable assistance

ISBN 0-7119-3030-0
Order No.OP46960

Exclusive distributors:
Book Sales Limited,
8/9 Frith Street,
London W1V 5TZ, UK.

Music Sales Corporation,
225 Park Avenue South,
New York, NY 10003, USA.

Music Sales Pty Ltd,
120 Rothschild Avenue,
Rosebery, NSW 2018, Australia.

To the Music Trade only:
Music Sales Limited,
8/9 Frith Street,
London W1V 5TZ, UK.

Photo credits: Dominick Conde/Starfile: 27; Mike
Guastella/Starfile: 78; Steve Judit/Starfile: 26c, 79b;
Todd Kaplan/Starfile: 56t; Ken Katz/Starfile: 73; Brett
Lee/Starfile: 87; London Features International: 7, 8,
11b, 12bl&br, 14, 15, 18, 19t&b, 20, 22b, 24b, 26b, 28,
33, 34, 37, 38, 41b, 42, 43t&b, 50, 51, 53, 55, 62, 63,
64t, 66, 67b, 68t, 72, 80, 81b, 93, 94, 95, 96; Jeffrey
Mayer/Starfile: 59; Laurie Paladino/Starfile: 41t;
Pictorial Press: 6, 9, 10, 16, 17, 21, 29, 31, 32, 36, 39,
40, 45, 46, 52, 56b, 60b, 61, 69, 74; Michael
Putland/Retna: 5; Retna: 4, 30, 67t&c; Rex Features: 12t,
25, 35, 64b; Gene Shaw/Starfile: 3, 60t, 88; Starfile: 44,
47, 49, 68b, 83l&r, 84; Vinnie Suffante/Starfile: 13, 22t,
23, 24t, 26t, 48, 54, 65, 70, 71, 75, 76, 77, 81t, 82,
85t&b, 89, 90, 91, 92; Frank Ziths/Starfile: 11t, 79t.

Printed in the United Kingdom by BPCC Hazells
Limited, Aylesbury, Buckinghamshire.

Every effort has been made to trace the copyright
holders of the photographs in this book but one or two
were unreachable. We would be grateful if the
photographers concerned would contact us.

A catalogue record for this book is available from the
British Library.

Contents

Introduction

Born and raised in Los Angeles, Cher was a teenager when she first became a household name twenty five years ago as half of the most successful male / female singing duo of the sixties.

Few performers have risked as much artistically with greater frequency or success than Cher. At various moments in her career, there have been those who have said that Cher could not do something. She could not be a singer. She could not be a television star. She could not be an actress, and most recently she could not have a hit album in the Nineties. Each and every time a determined Cher has proven them wrong.

This book focuses on her outspoken views on just about everything from men to politics, and music to movies. During her dazzling career over four decades no one has been quite as outrageous or as controversial, and many of Cher's quotes have been collectively captured… some of which may surprise you, and some may even shock! All of them make fascinating reading and are essential to understanding who Cher is, and what she has become.

But how much of the real Cher is revealed here and how much is pure public image. Is she a one-of-a-kind force in American culture? Is she a survivor with no nonsense? Or is she just plain and honest? Reading through what follows is the only way to judge her past, present and maybe, future.

This book is as good an observation as any biography could offer, with one telling advantage, they are all her own words…

"I wanted to be famous. I didn't know what it was going to be, I just wanted to be famous. And when I was famous, I just wanted to be good at something"… Read on!

Nigel Goodall.

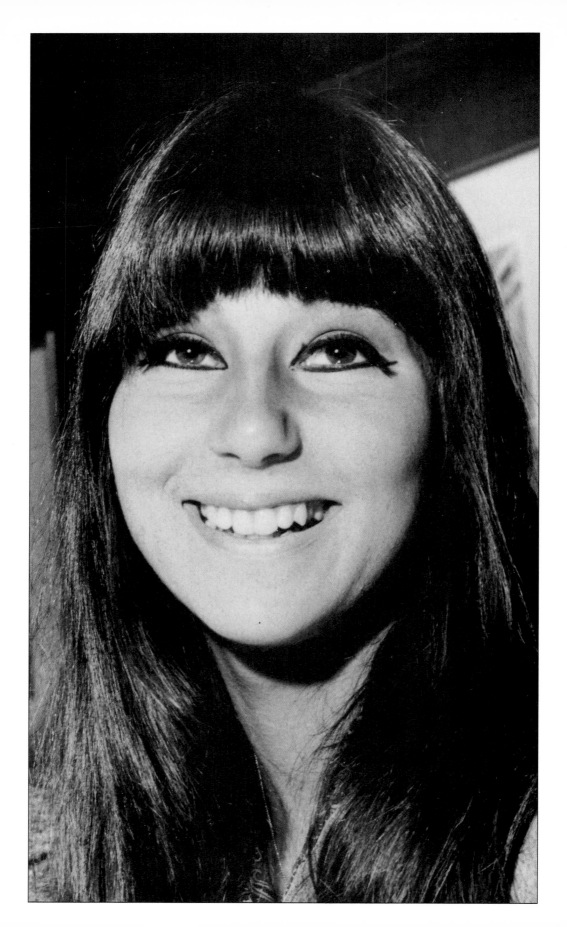

Growing Up

Cher with her mother, Georgia Holt.

**I walked away from home when I was sixteen.
I ran away when I was about four. 1992**

Family

I started out life in a very strange way. My mother and my father separated when I was really young, and my mother went back east and my father then met her, and he left, and she had no money and she put me in a Catholic orphanage. Then when she went to get me out, they wouldn't let her have me, so I was in there for, like, I don't know, eight months, a year, and after that I was in two different foster homes, so I really didn't live with my mother until I was about three and a half, or four years old. So, I think that was a much more traumatic effect on my life than by the time I was four and living at home, I think, even though it was strange, it was much more comfortable. **1992**

Cher with her sister, Georgeanne La Piere, June 1984.

One day my mother said, "Would you like to meet your father", and I went "Sure". And he came walking in and it was great because I didn't look like, I mean, I looked like my dead grandmother and my father. I didn't look like anyone in my family. So my father came walking in. I thought that's why my mother looks at me so strangely sometimes because he and I have the same expressions, you know. We have the same habits in some kind of strange ways, and I never even met him. But when he came walking in, I thought he was great. I thought he was very handsome and he was dressed really nicely and he had a great personality. He's very sweet but he has no character, but he's dead now but he had no character but he had lots of gratiating things about him. But he just really… he couldn't really get out of the life. He'd been in jail, he done lots of, you know… illegal things, and he just couldn't quite leave it behind him. **1992**

I was poor when I grew up, and I couldn't bear that. Before getting a chance to tell people what I had to say, they would know I was poor by the way I looked. I was ashamed. I felt that somehow it was my fault. I didn't understand it but I figured it was something I was doing wrong.

When I was little, my mother used to say, "Oh, I wish I could find someone nice, so we could settle down and have a normal everyday life!" And I used to think "Boy, I hope that doesn't happen!" Because the way we lived seemed like so much more fun. Maybe it was crazy, but it seemed like fun. **1982**

I used to daydream a lot as a kid. I still do. I'm always the heroine of whatever I think about – and everything always turns out really good.

When I was little, I wanted to be famous. I didn't know what it was going to be, I just wanted to be famous. And when I was famous, I just wanted to be good at something.

I remember about – being about six years old and hearing my grandmother and my mother

Cher with her daughter, mother and sister.

whispering about – "Well, you know, she's your daughter and she'll grow out of it", and I'm almost 45 and I haven't grown out of it. **1990**

I was this kid who came from no place. Not particularly attractive, not particularly talented. But I had something. **1991**

Even as a small child, I was always in my mum's make up and lipstick and dresses and stuff like that. **1991**

My mother… in some ways she was really great, she was very supportive and I wasn't very good at school and so she kept saying you know, well, don't worry about it, you know, you'll be able to do something else and I wasn't very pretty and she said, oh don't worry about it, you know, she was pretty supportive. **1991**

My mother was working in an all-night diner and had nowhere to put me. It was tough. She moved me from place to place while she was doing these kind of jobs. I think that's why I have a hard time staying with anything for too long a time now.

My mother and I haven't gotten along for almost my entire life. We always fought; we've always not talked, we've always argued. My mother is crazy, and so am I, but my mother is very special.

We're the youngest looking family of women I know. We have a tradition of having our first born very early. My grandmother is only 75 – she had my mother at 13 – and they both look amazing. So I'm hoping genetics are on my side. **1990**

I actually raised my sister and that's why I think she's so normal and good. **1990**

My mother and my sister and I have basically the same voice. My mother and I sing, my sister doesn't, but my mother was very glamorous for a mother, for a mum, she didn't really look like a mum, like in *Mermaids*, Mrs Flax is not very mum like, she's more like, I don't know what to say, she's much more like my mother. **1991**

It's a kind of a shame, but my mother and I had a real stormy relationship my whole growing up life, but mostly it would always come back to "be good". And lately, it's just – you know, it's not that I don't love her, I just don't really – I can't really talk to her and I can't really connect with her and so, it's just – you know, I'm kind of at a loss, so I just leave her alone. **1991**

I have a much better relationship with my mother now, but it's very strange. My mother forced me to be her mother for my whole life, and it really finally got on my nerves and now, at least it's very out in the open and it's very… I don't mind being her mother any more. **1992**

Chas is not close to her father now that she's grown up. She was very close to him growing up and Elijah's never been close to his father. He sees him, but he doesn't really know him. It's a sad thing because I think Gregory would have got an awful lot out of Elijah, but it just wasn't meant to be. **1992**

On Being A Mother

It's hard, being a mother, you have to remember that you are a mother, even when you want to do something that's not exactly "motherly". I felt kind of guilty splitting and saying "I'll see you in three weeks", but I knew she would be with her Dad, and I wanted to do it. I wanted to go away. If Chastity hadn't accepted it the way she did, I don't know if I would have done it, but she was real cool about it.

Chastity is like I am – pretty independent – but we're very close. I think it's important that she eventually has her own career and I trust her values and judgments a lot. The truth is she's a lot more level headed than me. **1990**

Chastity is the nicest person I know. We had about 45 minutes one summer where we had this kind of struggle between ourselves as

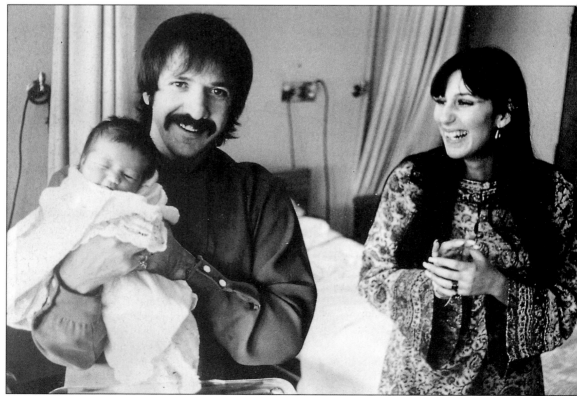

Sonny and Cher with daughter Chastity, 1969.

Cher with Chastity (top) and her son by Gregg Allman, Elijah Blue (below).

mother and daughter. I have more of a struggle with my son. He is much more like I am, more rebellious. **1990**

I think raising Elijah has been more difficult than raising Chas and I guess it's because I always feel like I'm not doing the other part of it. You know, I'm not being the – I'm not the father. So, I mean, I do the best that I can being the mother, but I'm sure that it would be better if he had a father too. **1990**

I was with Elijah not so long ago and we went to L L Bean and I wanted to get him a pair of boots and he wanted another pair of boots and I kept saying, "But they're – what you want is stupid. I know you," you know. "From your past history, you don't like to lace up your shoes. So, why don't you get the slip-ons", and I got really angry because he wouldn't do what I wanted and I realised that it's not his obligation to do what I want. **1990**

I think I've been lucky enough to play two mothers who love their children and are having

Top: Cher, Chastity and Sonny Bono;
below left: with Elijah Blue; below right: Dweezil and Moon Unit, son and daughter of Frank Zappa.

Elijah Blue and Chastity.

a hard time with them. And I know from being a single mother myself that you want to do your best. You try but sometimes you are not equipped. I mean that line in the movie (*Mermaids*) – "You guys don't come with instructions" – that's my line. **1990**

I am an unorthodox mother, and I made loads of mistakes bringing them up. Just like my mother made lots of mistakes bringing up me. **1991**

I think I embarrass my children. I think it's a mother's duty to embarrass their children. **1991**

I think people have kinda caught up to us, you know. Moon Unit and Dweezil (Frank Zappa's children) and lots of people have got names now that make my kids' look conventional. **1991**

I think I'm, in my own fashion, a good mother, you know. It's not exactly like everyone else's, possibly, but my children know that I'm there for them, and they know that I love them and I think that that's – you know, it's really an important thing in my life. It's like it's really – I was thinking the three best nights of my life were having my children and getting the Academy Award, so – and I think that liking yourself is really difficult and I think that's my goal because all the stuff that we do is more to hide ourselves than it is to like ourselves. **1991**

I would like to have one more baby 'cause mine are like, what, 22 and 15. **1991**

Making It

Sonny and Cher model interesting matching outfits in London.

Our big dream was to walk into a store dressed in blue jeans
and buy a Rolls Royce. All we cared about was spending.
We're both compulsive buyers. Sonny owns seven
cars and I buy clothes constantly. 1971

The Early Days

Sonny's lifestyle was so exciting. It was so interesting and I felt so great being a part of it, and I really liked him very much, and acting was something I was sure I could do anyway. **1992**

I have got more self confidence in the past twelve months, and I suppose more mature. Although I don't think I have changed or let things affect me in the way some people do when they get successful. **1966**

I didn't object to Sonny running things. He was better at it than I was. But I think people, including women, should have more freedom about how your life is run than just saying yes. **1974**

Hippies thought we were square. Squares thought we were hippies.

We were really poor, always planning how Sonny and Cher could make it. But nothing was going right for us in the States. We had these managers who lived in the prop room on one of the big motion picture company lots and they went round in prop clothing, which we had to borrow too. The only reason we could afford to make 'I Got You Babe' was that they hawked all this film equipment. I don't even know if it was theirs. So we took the song to London, which was where the music scene was really happening and maybe also because we looked a bit too weird for America at the time. When we got to England, we got famous… and then we went back to the States and everybody thought we were English, so we got famous there too. **1985**

London in the sixties was the best time. We met everybody: The Stones, The Beatles, Dusty Springfield, Sandie Shaw and that drummer guy Dave Clark. It was an incredible time. **1985**

When we first started people got really upset by it. We looked strange, but I don't think we were really outrageous. Most people at that time were very conservative: The Beatles were nice clean cut boys in their little round necked suits and only The Stones looked really wild. **1985**

Going hungry never bothered me – it was having no clothes. **1985**

I didn't really know how to do anything. I had no skills and I was terribly shy. I couldn't even call Information (Directory Enquiries) for mother, but I still wanted to be famous. **1985**

After 10 years, Sonny gave up trying to be a lead singer, deciding it was never going to happen for him. I thought, of course it will. It never really occurred to me that you couldn't do something you wanted to do. **1985**

In The Beatles' time you could be the world's worst singers and get to the top if you were English – which lots of Americans thought we were. Trying to make sense of success is senseless because it makes no sense. **1985**

When I met Sonny – I had moved out of my house when I was 16 and I was pretty independent, not completely independent, but I had – I was – had those kind of leanings, you know, and then I met Sonny – I got out in the world when I was 16 and I found it was a really difficult place, I really wasn't prepared for it. Sonny was 28 and he was very – really very funny and really weird and he was very – you know, he'd been married, he had a child and he just kind of took me under his wing. I mean, we were room mates in the beginning. I remember one night this girl came – I was – we were sleeping in twin beds and he didn't really find me very attractive – I mean, that was the truth of it – because I was really skinny and it wasn't too popular at that point and I remember hearing a knock at the front door. He went to it and two girls came in and saw me in the other bed, they were real surprised and disappointed and Sonny said "Well, you'll just have to come back tomorrow and she'll – she can go out for

The Beatles in 1965.

Above: The Rolling Stones.

the night or something". So when I got with Sonny, I was – I think I just wasn't really prepared to be out. **1990**

Later Years

What I always wanted, but Sonny got me to give it up soon after we met, and then things just seemed to go their own way. One day it struck me again that if I didn't make some real concerted effort to act, my chance would slip away. **1985**

Everything I'd done, I'd gone absolutely to the top of the field but no one who made movies gave a damn. There wasn't one studio head I didn't see – I tried for eight years and got absolutely no encouragement. Nobody wanted what they thought was Cher – and I thought my life would be worthless if I couldn't try my talent, not the stuff I was doing with my act. I was really dying in Vegas, just dying. I wasn't respected by anyone I respected. **1985**

It's a real pain in the arse what happens to some people in Hollywood.

Men

Men are luxuries, not necessities.

Men were something that you knew were around, but you couldn't quite figure out what their function was. And you could do without them easily – and most of the women I knew as a child did. All of the women who were my mother's friends were working women, they all supported their children alone.

I like men a lot. I have a sense of humour about myself. I don't care if people pose nude for *Playboy*, so I don't know if I'm a feminist or what. I don't really want to be anything. I don't like labels and I don't like labelling other people. I respect people for who they are, and I don't care if they're not like me.

I think it's a specific kind of man that is attracted to me or that I attract or that I'm attracted to. **1991**

I'm still friends with all my exes, apart from my husbands. **1991**

I like kind of street men. I like men with 1940's sensibilities. **1991**

Cher with Richie Sambora and (below) with Les Dudek.

When I like a guy, he's the last person in the room I'll talk to. **1991**

I am without a boyfriend at the moment. But I don't think there's anything missing. I'd rather be with someone than not, but not being with someone doesn't leave any gaping holes. **1991**

I haven't really had a lot of heartbreak with men, I mean at least not with ones that weren't my husbands. **1991**

Men are sometimes very scared of successful ladies and beautiful women, because the ones that are intimidated aren't the ones who come up to you. I guess that could be said for anyone. Most men don't come up and talk to me. **1991**

I have English men who are friends but I've never had an English man for a boyfriend. **1991**

I've been really happy with men but I think it's much better to be with the right man than to be with someone just because you're afraid of being without a man. **1991**

I don't need a man. But I'm happier with one. I like to have someone I can touch and squeeze and kiss. But I don't fold up and die if I don't have a man around.

Sometimes I find I have to make the first move because some men seem to be frightened of me. **1992**

I am 45 years old and I'm having a mid-life crisis. I haven't been with anybody for a year and a half. **1992**

I'm not attracted to that many people and I haven't seen anybody that I like that much. **1992**

I could most probably go for a couple of special ones. **1992**

I've been kind of alone for about a year, maybe a little more than a year. I do like my relationships but it was great for me. It was really a great thing for me to be alone this year, year

and a half. It was one of the best things that could have happened. I'm kind of in a relationship. I'm starting a relationship right now, but I'm not telling with whom. After being alone for what, gosh, a year and a half in August. That's long enough time to be alone. He's a very twinkly kind of person. He's the oldest man I've ever been out with. He's nine years younger than I am. **1992**

Young Men

Younger men are more fun to be with and they have a kind of softness I like, would you rather have a 23 year old boy who can hold you all the time and give you all the passion and love you need, or a 47 year old fart of a studio executive who leaves the house at 6am, works till 10pm and has nothing left for you at the day's end? **1990**

Younger men are more supportive and a lot less demanding, and they also have more time for their relationships. I want somebody who still wants to go dancing and spend the day at Disneyland, somebody who'll give me more than the little time he has left over after his day at the office. **1990**

With Jon Bon Jovi.

Top: With US TV host Dick Cavett;
below: Warren Beatty.

These younger men have been very loving and very supportive, and that's what's really important to me. I don't need a man to do anything else for me. **1991**

My mother lived with a guy that was – he was really young. He wanted to get married and my mother didn't. She left and went up to Santa Barbara, but I think he was like 20 years – he was a year younger than me. **1991**

I really hate the phrase toy-boy. It's so demeaning. **1991**

I want someone kind of fiery and street – yeah. **1991**

Older Men

Older men never ask me out. I tend to fall for guys who pay me attention – and they're usually the younger ones.

I don't particularly care for older men as a group.

Older men don't ask me out. I'm certainly not crying about it and I haven't the time to think about what the reasons might be, in fact, I haven't been with an older man for so long I

wouldn't know what it's like. Younger men have been very loving and very supportive. It's not a problem for them – so why should it be for me? I remember my mother living with a man a year younger than me, so it must run in the family. **1990**

I was figuring out the oldest man I've ever been with was Sonny and he was 40. Older men just never ask me out. Not that I care, they just don't. I never really thought about this until people started asking. I've only ever been out with one older man but he was married. **1991**

I think older men are a little bit more intimidated. Younger men are really not. I mean, I'm not looking for age range. **1991**

I'm sure there must be great guys out there in their forties, but they never seem to approach me.

Warren Beatty

What a disappointment. Not that he wasn't technically good, or couldn't be good, but I didn't feel anything!

With rock mogul David Geffen.

David Geffen

When I first met him, Joni (Mitchell) was living with him making 'Court and Spark' and he was always in the studio and really into it and he was excited if Jackson (Browne) was writing something new. He was really involved. But now David doesn't run Geffen. We have a very strange relationship. I'm very close to him but it has nothing to do with our business. We're just close personally. **1992**

Gene Simmons

He was kind of too soft for me. Just very easy going. We didn't get married because it wasn't true love.

Robert Camilletti

I never felt that way about anybody and it was just a great relationship that didn't interfere with my work because most men just don't want to put up with your work. And Robert was really supportive and he thought it was great what I was doing and he was very supportive. **1991**

I thought he had the most beautiful face I'd ever seen. I just thought he was – actually, I was just looking at him because I thought he was really interesting. **1991**

Richie Sambora

Relationships come to an end for all kinds of reasons. Richie and I had our day. It's over now, but we're still friends. I wouldn't be seen dead with someone who was meant to have said the kind of stuff he supposedly said about me. He wouldn't do it, it's all lies. **1991**

Cher with Kiss bassist Gene Simmons (top) and Val Kilmer (centre). Bottom: Richie Sambora.

Val Kilmer & Robert Camilletti

Val left me and so did Rob, they were both really young and looking for their own identity. I'm a pretty big shadow to crawl out from under, but I'm close to them all, I really love them. It's my ex-husbands I'm not close to. There is no man in my life right now – I don't have time. But I'm not lonely, I have great friends. After 11 years of a boring marriage, I have fun. **1992**

With Rob Camilletti.

Marriage

With Sonny during the Sonny and Cher Show in the seventies.

**Husbands are like fires – they go out
when they're left unattended. 1991**

I don't think marriage really suits me. To me marriage is for 5 or 10 years, whereas for others it's for a lifetime. That's not the best attitude to have. But is there any reason I should marry? Men don't have to be a good provider or offer security; so far as I'm concerned. I can do that for myself. **1990**

I'm not ruling out marriage. It's not completely out of the question for me ever again. I don't know. You know, I wouldn't mind doing it if I found someone I wanted to be with for a really long time. I've also been thinking a lot about babies. Time ticks away – and it's either put up or shut up. I'd love to have more children, it's the fundamental care of being a woman, I'm not doing it any more is admitting to being too old. **1990**

Maybe I'll marry again one day. I'm not looking for it but I've certainly nothing against the idea. **1992**

It's going to take a really special person to make me want to get married. If I ever do or if I ever will. **1992**

Sonny Bono

I was with a friend of mine, a girl friend of mine, and another record promotion man, and we were in a place called KFEB which was a radio station on Hollywood Boulevard and we were sitting downstairs in this restaurant, and a whole bunch of guys were there… you know, disc jockeys and radio people and regular people too. And I remember that someone looked up and said, "Ah! There's Sonny" and they said, "Sonny, come and sit over here with us". I turned over to where they were looking and I saw this strange man, and everyone kind of disappeared in the restaurant – I just saw him. He was… he had long hair and he was dressed really weird, and he had black high heels boots on, and he was just the strangest person I'd ever seen. He came over and sat down and everybody… he was really popular. He was the promotion man's promotion man, and everybody loved him. And I just kind of looked at him… and he liked my girl friend. **1992**

He was the strangest man I'd ever met and there was something interesting… but I lived in his house for a long time and nothing ever happened between us. He had girls coming in at all hours of the night and day and all that. We were just kind of friends. **1992**

One night I was having a bad dream. We lived in the same bedroom in twin beds, and one night I had a really bad dream, and I woke up and I was really frightened and Sonny got in bed with me and we just laid there and then I fell asleep. Then we went to a movie, this ridiculous movie. It was not romantic at all, and he held my hand and I thought, "That's strange… that's nice", and then my mom made me come home right after that and go with her on a trip, and Sonny just flipped out when I left and I really missed him. I thought, "What is this?", you know, because Sonny was 28 when I met him and I was 16, and all his friends thought I was this country dumb girl he was letting hang around. So anyway, when I left he just – he wrote me a letter and he called me on

the telephone and he said, "Don't you think that you like me?" I said, "Yeah, I do". He said, "Well, I miss you a lot". I said, "Yeah, I know. Isn't this weird?" and when I came back we just got together. I wish I could remember the actual night but I can't. I just know that we were friends for a long time, and he thought I was a real pain in the ass, and then all of a sudden I had to leave to go on this vacation with my mother. He was just totally miserable and lonely. And I lost all his clothes because when my mother used to come to the apartment, I would throw all of his stuff out of the back window and into my friend's apartment, but I lost almost all of his clothing by doing that. **1992**

I was crazy about him in the beginning.

The difference between 16 and 18 at that age is so... he'd been married (and) I'd never had very many relationships. He was living on his own.

I'd just moved out of my mother's house and when I met him I'd been really sick and I was kind of weak, so he just started out really by taking care of me... that's the relationship we had. He took care of me and... it became different. He took care of everything and I just kind of got used to saying "Yeah". And even as I started to grow older, he never saw me as growing older. He always saw me as 16. He always saw me as the baby. So it was very difficult to grow up around him. He just wasn't interested in that at all. He wasn't interested in my growth. He liked the idea that he was in charge of everything. **1992**

My mother had great hopes for me and she wanted me to be a great actress, and she thought that I could be... and then Sonny was 28 and divorced and just a promotion man, and my mother had these wild ideas that I would be something special, and that if I got with Sonny it would all be dashed. **1992**

He's the world's most untidy man. He leaves his clothes scattered all over the house. Yet he hates untidy people! He doesn't have a suit, and won't wear one now on principle. We could go a lot of places and meet a lot more people if we chose to conform. But we prefer to go our own way. **1965**

I don't have any regrets about getting married. I married Sonny because I wanted to and there's never been a day when I wished I hadn't. **1965**

Do you know what happened when I first took him home? My mother came into the room, looked at him, then took me out and said "What's that supposed to be?" **1965**

Our kitchen isn't one of the most modern things. I guess the only modern thing we've got

in it is the garbage disposal unit. Anyway, I hate cooking, so I'm not all that sad about the cooker. Sonny does all the cooking – Italian stuff. **1965**

Sonny and I both want kids. But it won't be for about two years because there's so much going on now. I wouldn't give up singing whatever happened – we'd take the kids with us wherever we went. **1966**

We want twins and I'd dress them like small versions of us with little furry jackets! I don't feel mature enough to cope with kids just yet.

They're cute but need a lot of understanding and I don't have that to give just yet. **1966**

Our marriage is different. We're best friends. When we go out on stage, sometimes I hold his hand or something. **1966**

I wasn't in control of anything. I was delighted for Sonny to take care of everything, I thought he was the tower, pillar of strength and maturity and intelligence. **1967**

I met Sonny when I was 16. He was 12 years older than me. I think he's probably a good husband now, but then he was terrible. When we did *The Sonny and Cher Show* he was always the nice one because he didn't want to appear high powered. He thought that was wrong for his image. Really Sonny was dictatorial, unfaithful, demanding, even though he was always a great partner. He was so Sicilian, so rigid. And I stayed with him for 11 years. **1990**

I didn't even like him that much. I just thought that he is the weirdest looking man I've ever seen. I mean he was ugly.

Sonny was – he seemed to know really so much about life that I just didn't know so I got into this really bad trap that, I think, women before me had to even grow up in and women now don't seem to and I think it's terrible for men too because women who can't be who they really are really kind of Machiavellian and deceptive and covert. It's like – one reason I thought I might never get married again is I was in Palm Springs and this woman was there with her husband. Obviously they were married and she wanted this dress really badly and she was – she had it on and she loved it and he didn't so she didn't get it and she was going through this "Oh, Daddy. Oh, Honey". And I was thinking, "Oh please. Up yours". I mean, this chick probably works on her hands and knees scrubbing bathtubs and like that and she's got to go "Oh, Daddy, can I have this dress?" **1990**

Of all the people I've ever been with, he's the person I know the least. I spent 11 years with him and I have no idea who he is. **1991**

I was never so alone as the eleven years I was married to Sonny.

The night I left Sonny, I was literally going to jump off a balcony. Sonny and I had been everyone's darling couple. I was afraid of what everyone would think. And when I left Sonny, he said, "America will hate you". I said, "I don't care". It had gotten to a terrible point. I weighed ninety pounds and I was literally going to jump. I thought: "Cher why don't you just leave him instead? I don't know why you don't think of things like that sooner". I guess it's why battered wives don't think, just pick up and go. It took a long time to pick up after that.

Immediately after I left him I was thrilled and delighted. I had the best time. It was great. But I didn't know what would happen to me career-wise, because with *The Sonny And Cher Show* we were America's sweethearts and I thought I was throwing it all away. **1992**

It takes me way too long to make any kind of change in my life. To make a big change, I have to be really uncomfortable and I had to get to a place where I really didn't care about anything. But it was hard even then because one thing that we always did was have a great working relationship and he was very funny. He'd be really cute and then I wouldn't be sure again. I was 16 when I met him and was with him for 11

years so I didn't have a lot of background as to what a long-term relationship should be or what my role should be in it. He was 28 when we met. I was more like his daughter than his wife. **1992**

I think in the beginning he did love me, but I think after a while, when we became famous, I was just… he didn't want me to go any place, he just wanted me to be there under his thumb. Now I know… after I left Sonny… what love is. It's not what he did. He was so frightened that I might go away and he wouldn't be able to be Sonny of Sonny and Cher… which is what happened in the end anyway. **1992**

With Gregg Allman.

Gregg Allman

I'd never been… even though I was in rock'n'roll, I'd never been… Sonny just wouldn't allow it. I never knew musicians, I was never really allowed to be around what was going on unless it was work. And I met Gregory and he was just… he was like this rock'n'roll prince. He just kind of came out of nowhere and he just dazzled me with his footwork. He was unbelievably charming and Southern, and gallant and that energy… the magnetism between us was just… it was immense. **1992**

I think I married Gregory because I was tired of having someone to tell me what to do that I chose someone who couldn't even tell himself what to do, and couldn't try to be dominant over me. **1990**

I didn't know he was an addict until four months after we were together, because I was working all the time and he was back and forth and I didn't really know. I'd never been around anyone who did drugs, so I was pretty much in love with him by the time I found out and then, of course, I thought, "Well, it's simple. If he wants to quit, I'll help him", (which is) what a lot of women have thought, I guess. It was traumatic and exciting, and a good thing to do when you were young. **1992**

I filed for divorce at ten days, but I didn't actually divorce him. We were married a couple of years. I didn't live with him. We were married for two or three years, I think. **1992**

I started to get a better idea of what life with him would be like. I said, "Oh Christ", you know… "I don't know if I can do this". I left him a million times because every time he would go back to taking some substance or other. I would leave and then he would call me and say, "I can't live without you. I want to stop. Come and get me". It was real… just like a movie. **1992**

I don't dislike Gregory, I actually like him, he's really a good person. A lot of problems, but a really good person. **1991**

I wasn't fully aware of what I was getting into. And we were in love, I guess. Gregory is the sweetest person but he has a lot of problems. **1992**

I truly loved him and I was devastated when we broke up. But we should never have married in the first place. We were too different. **1992**

He didn't manipulate me. I loved him because there's a certain side of Gregory that's like Elijah. It's brilliant. It's almost worth it but not quite. **1992**

I was put off Sonny and Gregg forever, but not men. **1992**

Music

The evolution has been gigantic.
I don't know if it's been better. 1992

Phil Spector, the first producer to stamp his own identity on the records he made.

Starting out on backing vocals with Phil Spector

I started on 'Be My Baby' and finished on 'You've Lost That Loving Feeling' and I did everything in between, including the Christmas album.

It was such a different time. It was nothing like now. It was like living on the earth and being brought up on the moon. The record business, rock 'n' roll, wasn't an industry then. I remember being with Brian Wilson and The Byrds – we hung out at Gold Star Studios – and it was like, the music was made by the young people and the older people just didn't get involved because they didn't really know what it was. They didn't get it. And the young people didn't know how much they were worth or how important they were as artists.

The last thing I did (for Spector) was the infamous Christmas album and I was the youngest person on it. I was pretty naïve then. I just couldn't understand why everyone else could stay awake for a month without sleep… I was nearly dying. I didn't realise they were taking just about everything there was to stay awake. I was only 16. **1985**

I have such a distinctive voice. You can hear it if you listen closely. I had to stand five feet behind everybody else when we were recording because my voice just wouldn't blend. It kind of cut through. It got to be a joke in the studio. "One more step back, Cher!" But, I can always hear my harmonies. **1992**

The first time I sang was on 'Be My Baby'. Darleen Love was late for the session. Phil Spector just looked at me and said, "Sonny says you can sing. I need another voice and we can't wait any longer. So get out there". **1992**

The evolution has been gigantic. I don't know if it's been better. I came into the business when they just had got into 4-track and everybody was like out of their minds, you know, because they used to do it mono, they used to have one track and put everything on it. It was just different, it was a lot more fun, it was a lot less business, you know there wasn't – people weren't so interested because no one knew what a gigantic money making thing it was going to be, so there weren't too many pseudo people in the area. **1992**

As a singer it was very difficult, because when I started singing I didn't sound like the women, I could never really sing along with the women, and the men were a little bit too low so, I really liked the women's voices, but my voice just didn't fit there so it wasn't that easy for me. **1992**

Sonny Bono

He learned a lot working with Phil Spector when he sang backing for The Ronettes. Now he does everything himself. He conducts, arranges, composes and produces all our songs.

He can't read a note of music but he has a perfect ear for the sound he wants. **1965**

Music is the most important thing to him – next to me. I think he's so good because he never writes anything unless he feels it. The first record we made 'Baby Don't Go' he wrote just after we were married. We were broke. 'I Got You Babe' he wrote after we were thrown out of a restaurant in Los Angeles because of our clothes. He knows what being hurt means and he puts real feeling into his songs. **1965**

I always liked what Sonny was writing about. I thought it was kind of appropriate, and yet I'm not so much proud of the creative part, or my part of it, but we were a really interesting team. We were larger than the thing we were doing, because what we did wasn't that great. It's never going to go down as great music, but we made an impact on a generation, so we must have been doing something more than just singing.

Sonny And Cher

Sonny's earlier reactions to success were very much like mine… they were very naïve. We were very excited and everything was so new. Everything was so fresh, all so strange and we weren't prepared for it. I don't think anyone ever is, but literally we were overnight sensations. We came here (UK) and in a couple of days we were huge stars. I couldn't even remember some of the stuff. I'd see pictures from those times and I wouldn't remember how we'd taken them, or where we were, because all of a sudden we were huge, just huge. By the time we got back to America, we were giants. We left America being relatively unknown, came here (UK), became famous, went back, and everyone thought we were English. **1992**

Easy Beat is a gas. They have this live orchestra actually playing in a studio and it's on radio!

We expected Paul Whiteman to come on. We really loved that show – honest. **1965**

We're not folk singers, we just give our own interpretation of folk and pop songs and try to put our own personalities into them, like The Beatles. Jazz is the only field of music I'm not interested in at all. **1965**

England is great because you can be a hit overnight there. One day they've never heard of you, and the next day you've got a smash. They hadn't ever heard of us before we got there, really. But everyone's so record conscious. **1965**

What do we sing? We call it folk'n'roll – a sort of folk music with a rocking beat. But with a smile. Ours is happy music – we haven't any message to impart. **1965**

We went out and bought a piano one day, then we didn't have any place to put it so Sonny stuck it in the garage and it's been there ever since. **1965**

I personally was not very fond of Sonny and Cher music. From that period of my life there were only two albums that I liked. **1977**

We didn't write any songs together. Sonny wrote them, but you know, we were married when we said we were married and I got the songs that he wrote after we were married. Well, he didn't really write very many songs after we were legally married, so it sounds good in copy, but it's really nothing. **1990**

We worked as a team, as a professional team, so he didn't realise that I was just becoming more and more depressed. I wasn't sure what it was, and then one night I thought, "I have to leave this, I don't want to be Cher of Sonny and Cher. I don't want to be on TV. I don't want to be in Las Vegas. I don't know what I want but I know I don't want this". I told him (Sonny) out of the blue. He was shocked. **1992**

Early Sonny And Cher was the happiest time for us. **1992**

'Ringo I Love You' (single)

(Released under the name of Bonnie Jo Mason)

They didn't play it because my voice was so deep on it, they thought it was a guy singing 'Ringo, I Love You'. **1992**

'Allman And Woman'

My publicist said I couldn't possibly have a record without my name on it, so I fired the publicist.

'Cher'

I was really nervous at first. I didn't sing for about five years, not even in the shower. I would rather think of singing as a hobby. Singing is much more organic a feeling than acting for me. Acting is more about being prepared. That's not saying it's unemotional, but it comes from a different place. Let me explain it this way: you can be happy and sing around the house, but you can never be happy and act around the house.

I liked the idea of being able to be around long enough to make a copy of my own record of 'Bang Bang' some twenty years earlier. I don't think anyone else has ever done that. **1987**

'Heart Of Stone'

I wanted to have songs that really suited my taste. When I sing a song, they're always about me. That's not narcissistic. It has to be personal. I have to hear how it relates to me.

'Love Hurts'

All the songs that kept coming into this album were all either wishing you were in love songs, being in love songs, or being out of love songs and just kind of went together. **1991**

Actually I thought that I would not be able to sing these songs had I not had some heartbreak in my life and so I think I sing them from experience. **1991**

'The Shoop Shoop Song'

You could have just knocked me over with a feather because in America the song wasn't such a – I mean it wasn't a big hit at all, it was just an OK song, you know, but I was shocked it was number one for four or five weeks here in England. **1991**

'Love Hurts' (single)

I couldn't sing a song like that without kinda knowing the feeling. **1990**

Random Notes

I'm not the best singer in the world. I can't listen to my voice. I don't like it. You see all your mistakes when you hear your voice. You see all the imperfections.

I never thought my albums were very good, and I got upset that I couldn't sing the way I wanted to. **1987**

In this business it takes time to be really good – and by that time, you're obsolete.

I never thought I would want to do disco. People keep saying "There's no such thing as disco". It's like saying the world is flat! It's here… people should know it. It's terrific! It's great music to dance to. I think that danceable music is what tells everybody what's in.

A film is so much different from a song. One of my favourite songs is a Procol Harum song

called 'A Whiter Shade Of Pale' and I still have
no idea what that song's about. I have no idea
what they're singing about but I love the sound
of it. In movies you really have to go for the
dialogue and know what you're saying but in
songs you don't have to go so much for the
lyrics. **1990**

I'm 45 and suddenly I've discovered that I love
singing more than ever. **1991**

Concerts

I don't like going out to concerts much any
more. I'd be really excited to see Eric Clapton.
Or Etta James. I can't think of many people I'd
be really excited to see live. But I love Eric
Clapton's music and I love the history of his
music and I think he's a really great player, so
that would be something I'd want to spend
some time with. **1992**

Eric Clapton at the Albert Hall.

Stage

It's not enough to be good
– which is kind of sad –
but it's true

The Early Days

I hate that shut-up feeling. When you're on stage you know you've got to be there for the next 30 minutes whatever happens. **1966**

He's there to calm me down before we go on stage too. I love it all but I get this terrible feeling that I'm trapped directly I walk out into the lights. **1966**

I still rely on Sonny for everything. I couldn't appear on stage without him. I wouldn't want to sing without Sonny being there. You get used, you see, to someone to laugh with and look at and be on stage with you, and Sonny is all those things and more. **1966**

It's not much fun working without Sonny. When I wanted to ad-lib there was no one there. I'd rather have more fun and half the glory. **1975**

In the old days when I first started, I was terrified of the crowd. When we were doing the rock and roll shows and stuff like that, you never got to finish a song. You took the money and ran like hell.

Vegas

Las Vegas is my gig. That's how I pay my rent and my kid's schooling.

Las Vegas was not the happiest period of my life, because so many people were convinced that I couldn't do anything else. I am not satisfied when someone says, "You can't come and join us – you're not good enough", or "We don't want you; what makes you think you can do that?" So being in Las Vegas without any other outlet was terrible. I felt like I was in the elephant's graveyard.

I don't like Vegas very much. It was something I did because of work. It's not at all like doing concerts. Concerts are a blast. With Vegas it's work. It was my job. **1991**

The Broadway Stage

Being in a play is so different from anything that's ever happened to me before. There's an audience out there and yet you don't have to pay any attention to them, and it's wonderful. I much prefer it to nightclub work, where you have to play to the audience all the time. I don't really know what I'm doing most of the time onstage, and if I stop to think about it, I won't know what I'm doing at all. When we started, everyone was talking about preparation, and I didn't know what that was. What I do is sort of turn my mind to pretend. I thought I'd hate having to be the same character every night, but I found it was natural. There was a lot of freedom in it. **1982**

I'm threatened by Broadway. An artist isn't intimidated. **1982**

I have been so nervous with this play, my entire body chemistry was thrown off. I had to go to two doctors and they said my nerves have just totally fucked up my body.

Everyone's an actor in New York. These are the kind of things that a city like this offers that you just can't get anywhere else.

Working with Sandy Dennis is the thrill of my life. I've never worked with anyone in my life I've liked as much. I learn something from her

Cher with the cast of La Cage Aux Folles in New York.

every single night. I suck up all the things I see and I watch everything. **1982**

One night all the girls were talking about what they do for preparation, and I didn't say anything. So Sandy Dennis came up to me – we had this great relationship where she was always busting my chops – and she said, "Well, what do you do?" I said "I just put my make-up on. By the time I finish doing that, I'm late for my cue". When I get onstage, I just work. I don't know what the hell I'm doing and if I stop to think about it, I really want to know what the hell I'm doing. Everyone was telling me, "Girl, if you fall flat on your face on Broadway, the whole world is going to know about it". I guess I was just too stupid to know how awful it would be for my career if I was terrible. **1990**

Touring

When we came here, everyone was talking about the London Bus, and I thought there was just one big bus driving about. **1965**

I'm homesick. I want to go to the beach and eat hot dogs. I want to go to drive-in movies and sit and watch TV all night. **1965**

The first trip I was so afraid because it was so far away from home. And you're really away from home when you're there! But this time, since we've made a lot of friends, we're really excited and we're going to go all over. Now we know all the places to go and we're not strangers anymore. **1966**

The trip has been completely taken over by youngsters of about 16, all the clubs and everything. And they all walk around asking you what sign of the zodiac you were born under because it's so highly significant. We don't mind it but the older people don't like it at all. **1966**

The scene in Hollywood is very odd just now so we don't go out much. Everyone thinks it's very swinging and full of weirdos but really some of the people we've met here in Britain on this trip are far more way out!

When we returned from Britain last year we did a month's coast to coast appearances. I find it hard to cope with something like that. It was enough. Apart from that we've done about two concerts. The rest of the time we were filming, which was lovely and easy and meant we could spend a lot of time at home which we both like doing. **1966**

I do love it, I love it all. I enjoy being able to do so many things I like. Yeah, OK, I get sick of it sometimes. **1990**

People say "How can you stand a whole summer on the road with all of the one night gigs". Well, I thrive on it.

I am too old to be doing this. I doubt whether I'll do another road show. There comes a time... **1990**

The actual work of it is more uplifting. You can see the joy you bring at that moment.

I was terrible. I still don't have that self-confidence. It used to be really difficult for me. Sonny actually pushed me on stage the first time. I was real timid. **1992**

If I was a fan of me I would go and see myself, but I don't know if I'd be a fan of me. **1992**

I'm always thrilled when there are like days off. Whenever I see off I'm just so excited. **1992**

I don't like doing one thing all the time. It's like I'm getting real itchy to act again, I haven't done that in a while so this'll probably be the last time I tour for a really long time. **1992**

Television

I'm not ashamed of *The Sonny and Cher Show* at all. For a long time, it didn't matter to me. I never liked myself. I always thought I was a second-rater, a second-rate TV performer. At first all I wanted to be was famous; then I realised that fame had nothing to do with talent. I felt that I didn't do anything quite well enough, that I was one of those people who was famous but not very talented. So I said, okay, I'll be the Dinah Shore of the seventies, on TV all the time but nobody quite knows why. I was rich and famous and I had everything. I figured it was too much to ask to be talented too.

I changed really with, I think, the TV show. (Maybe) a little bit before the TV show, but the TV show really put it over the edge. I could grasp it a lot faster than Sonny could so he really looked at me for help. **1992**

Sonny and Cher with Jerry Lewis.

I'm kind of like queen of a mediocre medium. Television is the kind of thing you can pay attention to if you wish, and if you don't, you can go clean out your drawers. **1975**

Video

I made two videos that just couldn't get the time of day. They said, "It's not a Cher video, you have your clothes on the whole time". They wouldn't say that to Eric Clapton! **1992**

Doodles

It's not enough just to be good – which is kind of sad – but it's true.

Art is about stirring things up.

I'm never sure what I'm going to be able to handle and it's always kind of nerve-racking. You always want to do your best. **1990**

There were things I wanted to do, but I don't think about fortunes. I mean, I thought, "You make money. You lose money. It comes. It goes. That's the way it happens". I knew that I wasn't doing exactly what I wanted to do anyway, so I was working constantly. I was playing Las Vegas and I was playing all over the world and that kind of took my mind off it. I was doing concerts, but then it started to get really boring. I was happy in the beginning and then all of a sudden it just became my life. When I thought it was just a phase, I thought it was great, and then it became my life, then I hated it, so I stopped. **1992**

You know you're getting older when you walk out and everybody in the audience stands up. They're going to start trying to give me a lifetime achievement award pretty soon. **1990**

With Muhammed Ali.

Movies

I'm really a fine person and a dedicated actress
who wants to work hard and do good films.

Good Times

I get so excited about the story. It's like a book. I know it almost by heart, but I get a kick everytime I hear it. In the movie, I can tell you, I play a lot of different parts. So I'm having special wigs made. There will be period costumes, besides our whole wardrobe…

…Some of the wigs will be done up so it will look like short hair and they will be different colours too. I'm anxious to see how I will look because this is the only colour hair and only style I've ever had…

…With this wig, I have to spend two and a half hours in make-up every morning. They wash and dry my hair first, then wind it around my head and put on the wig. The lady curls it and so it all takes a long time. I don't mind though 'cause I can just sit there and let them work on me. The wig's not very hot, but kinda tight. After several hours, it gets uncomfortable, but usually I'm too busy to worry about it. **1966**

Sonny's getting such a kick out of doing this film. I'm glad we'll be doing two more. Most people think he just worries about my happiness and we do things to suit me. But I'm concerned about him too and I like to see him so enthusiastic. **1966**

Chastity

I remember going to a preview and seeing everyone laugh at the serious parts. I left crying and said I'd never do another film.

Come Back To The Five And Dime, Jimmy Dean, Jimmy Dean

I was in California going to those dumb auditions and Shelley Winters said, "Go to New York and get serious". I had just started studying with Lee Strasberg there when I got the part in *Come Back To The Five And Dime, Jimmy*

Dean, Jimmy Dean. I just kept going but having a movie career nearly killed me financially. We were bankrupt almost ten different times. Every month my business manager says we can't pay the bills. Fortunately, I've always bought things that save my arse, like apartment buildings or land that happened to have oil on it! **1990**

Silkwood

(It was) most fun doing *Silkwood* because Meryl (Streep) had all the responsibility and I didn't even know where I was supposed to stand. I was really ignorant and I just kind of floated, making jokes with the crew and having a good time.

Silkwood was a great movie and one of the most exciting experiences of my life. What an incredible cast I worked with and we became such a close-knit family. **1992**

Mask

Originally I didn't want to do something with this much responsibility so soon. I wanted to wait before I did a starring part, to bridge it with something. But when this came along, I didn't have a choice.

Okay, so doing it gave me a bit more confidence but not much really. My next project will make me just as fearful. **1985**

I don't think it's a perfect movie, but it has a real sense of Rocky's life, and of how incredible he was. All the people who knew him say he was a really fabulous boy with his strange lifestyle and his crazy mother. There are lots of faults in it, but I think it's a valid film. **1985**

It's the most rewarding feeling I had doing a movie. It was just something special and I've met lots of people it had a real profound effect on. **1991**

The director was just a complete arsehole, and he didn't really like me and one morning he came into my dressing room and he was eating a fried egg sandwich and it was very unattractive and he said, "You know Cher, I just want you to know something, this movie isn't about the mother, it's about the boy and I could cut you out", and I went "Yeah", and then he went on to say a whole bunch of other things, which I, even with my language, I'm sure I can't get away with this on English TV, so, and mostly he was saying, "If you think I want to do this, this, this, this and this with you, you're wrong". **1991**

When I did *Mask* they had wanted to get Jane Fonda and she didn't see it, you know, she didn't want to do it but when I saw it, it was like exactly perfect, it was like my cup of tea. It was something that I really wanted to do. **1992**

When I first read *Mask*, I cried so hard – I think for 45 minutes straight – I couldn't even talk to anyone. Rusty's relationship with Rocky was very much like the relationship I have with my own two children. It's very unconventional mother-child relationship, very loving but not typical parent and child. **1992**

Mask is still my favourite movie and the one closest to my heart because of the role of Rusty and the emotional drain it required. Sam (Elliot) was fabulous to work with. That movie more than any other marked a real turning point for me. **1992**

The Witches Of Eastwick

It was like filming a movie on Friday the thirteenth in the middle of a hurricane. But a movie doesn't have to run smoothly to be good.

Making *Witches* was a horror story but I came out of it with a great friend, Michelle (Pfeiffer), and a real nice friendship with Jack. He is unbelievable. He was up to his arse in *Batman* and *The Two Jakes* and he still remembered my birthday and Christmas. I loved the scene where he had to seduce and break me, and I had to tell Jack, he was a pig, he was vile, disgusting and smelled. That was fun. Except, it's kind of hard to do that – tell Jack Nicholson all those horrible things about him, even for a movie role. **1992**

Michelle Pfeiffer.

Suspect

It was disappointing. In my effort to be really
real, I was really boring. I wasn't embarrassed
but I wanted it to be more.

Working with Dennis Quaid in *Suspect*, I found
him very, very generous and sweet. **1992**

Moonstruck

As much as I liked it, it wasn't *Mask* which I felt I
had to do. I was a little frightened because there
seemed to be all kinds of possibilities and all
kinds of risks here.

It was too silly, too much like fun to be work. It
was like getting paid lots of money to have a
good time with a bunch of people you wouldn't
have minded spending time with anyway. **1989**

It was such an easy movie to make, it was really
fun. And it's hard sometimes when you're
making something that's really easy. You think
it can't possibly be this good, 'cause it's like
having a good time and getting paid for it.
1991

Cher with Nicholas Cage in *Moonstruck.*

I did *Moonstruck* in 1987, and one of the reasons I did it was because I was afraid to do it because I thought it might be bad for my career. I almost didn't do it because I thought it was so weird that no one would go and see it. But then I thought that the script was so good it didn't make any difference – if you do something as a piece of art and do a really good job of it, it'll be something that you'll be proud of forever. Either you are an artist or not. If you are, you take chances. **1992**

Moonstruck was so popular because I think everyone wishes times were gentler and easier, less complex and that people were most accessible. That's what it was about. I was never bored working with Nicky (Cage) and he does really weird things that kept me on my toes, though they sometimes pissed me off. Olympia (Dukakis) was fabulous, always open and searching for new things to do. **1992**

Mermaids

It's very reminiscent of *Moonstruck* – kind of a sweet look at people who are totally out of their minds doing the best they can. **1990**

Some people implied that I didn't take a starring role because I was frightened or something like that. I just thought it was a movie I could believe in, that I was willing to put a lot of time into and that I could do well. It had some meaning to me but it's a good thing I'm not in marketing. **1990**

It was a book and so there was a story, but I must say that the writer was much nicer about me in the script than Mrs Flax. I think Mrs Flax in the book is not nearly as nice or interesting and so she – they kind of moulded it a little bit so it would be better for me to do. **1990**

I actually based my character of Mrs Flax on my mother and I think that's what kind of really intrigued me when I was reading this – the first pages that I got of this script and my mother and my sister and I had basically the same relationship. **1990**

Mrs Flax is my mother. They are one and the same person. The dresses were taken from old Polaroids my mother had from the sixties. The dresses work. Mrs Flax doesn't have to open her mouth too much – look at her and you get a quick sense of who she is. **1990**

This is the closest character to me that I've played so far. **1990**

I'll see it when it comes out. I'll pop into a theatre and see it with people. **1990**

Mrs Flax is definitely her own woman in a time when that wasn't so easy. She goes her own way while everyone else is trying to look like Doris Day. **1991**

I actually play my mother… that's why I took this movie role because it was so similar to my youth experience, only I play my mother and Winona plays me, and that's kind of the reason I took it because my mother was really nuts and Mrs Flax is really nuts, and I had a little sister, my sister is still with me, she's not little anymore, she's 40, but still. **1991**

When I decided I wanted to do *Mermaids* I received a lot of offers but I didn't really like any of them and a lot of people thought I was wrong to do *Mermaids*, because it's such a small movie and it's still an ensemble piece, but I really wanted to do it. I like making movies that I really like. I hope I never have to make them for money. **1991**

Once the director got fired it was much better. The new director was really fabulous. Richard Benjamin was fabulous, but we were behind schedule by that time so we were always playing catch-up, but the first couple of months were rehearsal time and the first couple of weeks and month of shooting were really hard. **1992**

The Academy Award

It is an honour to be nominated, but the moment you don't win, you're a loser, so you go there as a nominee and everyone's going "Oh congratulations, it's great". And then when you lose, people kind of shy away from you. It's like they're embarrassed, they don't want to talk to you and so you just kind of find yourself wanting to sneak out of the building.

The night I won the Oscar, it was so bizarre because I was sitting there and when Paul Newman started reading the nominees, I just started going deaf, I mean, really deaf. And then, when he opened the envelope and he looked down at the paper, he took a breath and I thought, "Well, I didn't win because you don't need a breath to say Cher". I thought, "Oh, that's it". And then, he said "Cher", and I thought "Oh he said Cher". I guess he needed breath to say Cher. And then all I knew was that Robert was there and Chastity was there and they stood up and I didn't realise that the rest of the place stood up. I didn't really realise anything. The only thing I remember is I tripped on my shawl and I lost my earring and I was really pissed off...

...And then I remember getting up there and I'd been practising my speech for years in my shower, you know, like with my sponge and then, when I got up there, I didn't really expect to win really. Like in the back, back, back of my mind, I just thought it was going to be too much if I won, and so then, I just made up something at the last minute...

...It had been a really rough day and I mean, I'd lots of things that day. I'd done lots of work. And we were just so thrilled and so happy and my feet hurt and so we just went home and ordered pizza. We were all sitting around with the Oscar. Everyone was holding it...

...I gave it a lot of thought and I was thinking, you know, it's so difficult to say this was the best performance. I still have a hard time with that because I just don't think you can compare. I mean, great work is great work and I would have had a hard time picking, you know. I mean, some years it's more difficult and I was thinking a lot of it has to do with luck. I mean, a lot of it has to do with luck. I think I did a good job, but I think I was just extra lucky. **1991**

When I was little, my mother kept saying, "I want you to be something, and I guess the award represents 23 or 24 years of my work... and I never won anything from my peers before, so this means a great deal. I'm really, really happy. **1988**

Winning the Oscar meant success to me in a business where I had been considered a joke. It meant you could never say I wasn't talented. If you think about where my film career started and when and what I did and the space of time I did it in, it is pretty unbelievable. Considering that for *Mask*, the second film, they wouldn't even put my face in the posters or in the trailer because the studio was afraid people wouldn't accept me. When the picture became a hit they put my face on the posters. So I have come a long way. **1992**

Acting

When I saw Linda Ronstadt in *Pirates of Penzance*, I thought "Jesus, if she can be on the stage, then what am I doing!" I finally decided to study with Lee Strasberg. He said, "You've got to stop all of this nonsense and get serious". I decided to finally prove to myself that I was an actress.

I've never taken acting lessons except for a few, more than 20 years ago. And every director's begged me not to while I was working for him. Meryl (Streep) too – the world's best actress – said formal training isn't what I need. But my roles so far have fitted my personality because they've all been very kind of bizarre. **1985**

It was difficult for someone my age to get started as an actress, especially as there are so many good actresses in my age group. Why bother with someone who's untried and kind of freaky looking? And no one knows what you can do if you've never acted properly before. **1985**

Cher picks up her Oscar for Best Actress in *Moonstruck*, **April, 1988.**

Actually, I really wanted to act and everyone kept telling me that I couldn't be an actress because I was a singer so I just gave up. I didn't want to do it anymore because I really enjoyed being an actress and I hated the idea that I couldn't do both. People didn't really mean that. It was just their nice way of trying to dissuade me, to tell me don't do it. **1991**

I'd like to be an actress, but no one wants me to do it.

It's very tiring and tedious and it's like working in a factory with small parts. You have to have so much concentration it's just really not much fun.

It's ridiculous. People are too judgmental. I'm not any more serious now than I was before – when I was on TV, or when I was modelling for Vogue. Now that people like my work, they say I'm a serious actress.

There's a whole generation around who can only remember me as a film actress. But it wasn't easy – no one really gave me a hope of success.

There are already parts I can't do. I'm deadly serious about my work, but I'm not gonna become Ann Bancroft or Meryl Streep and have all the burden that being a "serious actress" entails.

I would die for another good film role and to receive another Oscar to prove to everyone that Cher is indeed a great, fine actress. **1992**

I wasn't strong enough to turn my back and say "I really want to act and I'm giving it all up to be dedicated". I probably should have. But I didn't. I didn't choose to… yet.

It's bizarre. I couldn't become an actress for five years because I was a singer. Then everyone was worried that people weren't going to accept me as a singer because I'm an actress. It's very funny because today a lot of kids are saying "Cher, the actress… she sings?" **1992**

Screen Scribbles

Thank God I wasn't in the Olivia De Havilland days. I would always have been on suspension.

It took me five years to get a job, but I don't think it had to do with being a woman. It's just people weren't really interested and I mean, men make more money in Hollywood and men make more movies and men have more control, but, you know, so what else is new. **1990**

I don't think making movies is – I don't know what the fun part is exactly, but I'm – I know that making movies – acting is the fun part, but you're only – you know, you get to do that 15 minutes in a day if you're lucky. So, you're just always sitting there trying to be prepared to be good when they say, "OK, now, and do it now and I hope you're feeling like you're going to be really good" and you go "Yeah, me too. I hope I'm feeling like I'm going to be great. **1990**

You get a script. You get lots of scripts and usually they're real terrible and then you'll be reading and all of a sudden you get taken away, and when you're taken away is when you know that that's the thing that you want to do and that's how – I just – I get – you know, if I start reading it and I become involved with it, then usually I end up doing it. **1990**

I hadn't been enjoying what I was doing for quite a while, and I wanted to try something else. I didn't regard it as a risk, launching myself as an actress. It was an opportunity, and a logical step for me. I thought that maybe I'd be talented in that area, but I wasn't sure and had to try. Eventually the right stuff came along and I had some success. **1990**

I really like to go to the movies and get popcorn and sit with people – you know, with people. **1990**

I felt that I had been completely slighted by the Academy for *Mask* and I thought – and one of the things that kept coming up in newspaper articles were, "Well, if she didn't date younger men and if she had a last name and if she didn't dress the way she dressed, maybe the Academy could take her seriously". **1990**

I turned down *Thelma And Louise* and I must say I'm happy for Susan (Sarandon) and I'm sure I would have done a good job of it, but it wasn't, you know, things are meant to come to you. I didn't like the idea of the ending very much. I don't know. The killing and the suicide, I don't know. I didn't believe so it was difficult for me. But does that mean it was a bad movie or does it mean that someone else couldn't see it and say "Oh absolutely, I totally believe in this", you know. **1992**

Sonny and Cher in *Good Times*.

Fashion

Somebody's got to do it. It's a dirty job, being ridiculous, but I'll do it. 1991

Clothes

I don't worry about the styles. I have my own,
I've been wearing the bell bottom pants for
several years and long before they came into
style here. I must like them. I haven't worn a
dress in a year and a half, because I like pants
better. **1965**

I like bell bottom pants too. We don't like
anything square. **1965**

A visual image is important. So many people
make a good record on the strength of their
voice, then they just drop off. It seems
necessary today to have visual popularity.
Sonny and I have always dressed this way, but
people said we should continue to do so when
we made it on records. **1965**

I do wear ordinary shoes too. **1965**

I remember the very first time I went and
bought a long dress. Sonny kept saying "You've
got to do it, you've got to change", so I went to
a store on Sunset Strip, and it was a terrible

store. I don't know why I went there, except
that it was the only place I could remember
that had long dresses in the window. **1972**

I love to dress up and go to big parties. It's fun
to see whose dress is prettiest. And usually
mine is. It just turns out that way. **1973**

When Sonny and Cher began, we used to
change into a suit and dress till one time our
suitcase didn't turn up and we went on in our
regular clothes, and people loved it. I think we
used to look fabulous, and we had a good time
dressing that way. You know when someone
said to Dolly Parton, "Don't you think you look
ridiculous?" she said, "When I get dressed up
and look in the mirror, I always think how
beautiful I look". It doesn't matter what people
think. But it was a problem for me when I
started trying to get a job acting. People
thought I couldn't be an actress because of the
way I've always dressed. **1985**

As you can see, I did receive my Academy handbook on how to dress as a serious actress. **1986**

The way I dress, the things I do and people think I do might be considered a hindrance to my career but they are not a hindrance to my life. It's like painting a big target on my arse and letting anybody who wants go for it. **1990**

I know why I spend so much money on frivolous things and clothes. When I was young, I never had any clothes. At one stage I went to school with elastic bands wrapped round my shoes to keep the soles together. **1990**

I do wonder how much longer I'll be able to dress the way I want to and get away with it. Will I be able to have long hair in another 15 years? Can I wear mini-skirts if my legs are still good enough. There are so many older women now who look good and don't feel ashamed to show it. There's been an attitude among some men – and women – for too long that age stops them from wearing or doing certain things. **1990**

I wear the tackiest clothes you can imagine. I mean, you know, I go around, no make up, scraggly. **1991**

I remember there was a time when I'd go into Bennis Edwards in New York and just buy, you know, 20 pairs of shoes and now, I look at all the shoes I want and then pick out of them the ones that I really want. I mean, I think that I'm growing up in certain ways. **1991**

Everyone thought the look was odd, but it caught on. That taught me to dress how I feel. One of my pride and joy outfits was red, white and blue striped bell-bottoms, and industrial pants zipper with a huge pull ring, and bell-sleeved blouse.

I love the way I look in those skimpy outfits and I feel comfortable in them. **1992**

We just thought it was different and cool. Sonny had long hair when I met him and he was the first person I'd ever met with long hair. **1992**

We were dressing like hippies before it really had a name. But we didn't live like hippies. We didn't do drugs, we didn't have a crash pad, didn't go to love-ins. We were just regular people. **1992**

I was so happy standing up there in an outfit which made me look like a Las Vegas showgirl. **1992**

Jeans and leather jackets. That may sound boring, but I can't resist them. I've got hundreds of them. I've always wanted to run a boutique selling wild funky clothes. **1992**

I always wore pretty little. I always been kind of a minimalist as far as clothes are concerned. **1992**

Another aspect of Cher's artistry.

Tattoos

You either love them, or are really disgusted by them and I can understand both things, but this is my life and I have to do what I want.

I honestly wish I hadn't started so early because tattooing is so refined now and a lot of my tattoos I don't really like that much, but they're with you forever. I can imagine when I'm like a seventy five year old woman with a tattooed body, it's gonna be really funny, and my flowers are down to my knee-caps or something. **1991**

Looks

My nose is not one of my favourite things. **1971**

I had my breasts lifted – not enlarged – after I had children because they'd got very big during pregnancy and never were before. One operation – and I talked about it openly because I'm open about everything, and I hoped I might make it easier for women with the same problem. **1985**

If I'd had some ribs out, wouldn't I have some scars or something like that? You know, you can't have surgery without having scars. No doctor can cover up scars, and if there is one who can, I'm sure every woman in the world would wanna know about it, 'cause then we'd all have the lot done. **1990**

I'm surprised that anybody got a date in the sixties. I really am. Actually, I – in my own terms, I'd say I'm a lot different than that, but I am surprised. I kept looking at myself and I was like a cross between that girl and an old Barbra Streisand movie. **1990**

I had the biggest nose in the history of the world. I didn't realise my nose was that big. On TV, it didn't look that big, but, you know, when you have a nose – when you've got close-up and it's like, what, you've got a four foot nose all of a sudden. I mean, I didn't like that. **1990**

You think I look wonderful? Well I spend hours in the gym sweating my ass off to look like this. This is all my skin. I've had these cheekbones since I was young, and the same chin. You know it's really ridiculous, and I'm tired of talking about it. But it seems that people would rather believe all that than truth. I'm fed up with defending myself because I don't really care. I guess I will always have to put up with the fantastic, supernatural stories about myself, me and Michael Jackson both. **1990**

I don't really think of myself physically. When I think of myself physically it's more as an instrument to do my work. When I'm not working I don't look in the mirror. **1991**

I think this way about it, it's my body and if I want to do it like Michael Jackson I will.

Am I obsessed with the way I look? Ooh... Do you know what I'd like to say to that? I don't give a flying fuck. **1991**

You can stand up for what you do, but it's really difficult to stand up for what you don't do. You know, it's like a couple of years ago, in a French magazine, they had arrows to all parts of my body that I was supposed to have had worked on and I thought it was so stupid that I didn't – I thought it was stupid. And then it came over to the States and I mean, I saw a woman on television once – I even made a call – she said she was going to have her ribs removed like what I had and it shocked me that someone would go and do something like that, thinking I had done it and I thought it was really... Well, I went to England and they had really never seen me perform over there and the audiences were so – like I would make a joke about it when I came that they would look at me like I was Robocop or something and there were really bad interviews done or articles done. And I ended up going to a doctor and saying, "Here, check me up and write down what you see and then let me send it in to the newspaper and say get off my case. He wrote down that, well, the reason it started is because I was doing an interview and this woman said, "And Cher looked at me with her surgically-enhanced gaze". And I said, "That's it". You know, I've had my teeth done, I've had my nose done, I've had my breasts done. I went to the doctor, I said "All right, now check me out everyplace", and I have a copy of the letter and I sent it to everybody. I mean, I don't even know that there is an operation that can

Over the years I've had my breasts done, my nose done and my teeth done. But I guess I always wanted to look in the mirror and see this blonde, blue-eyed girl. So no matter what I do I'm never going to be that. But I guess I've managed to come to terms with it by now. **1990**

remove your ribs. It wouldn't occur to me 'cause I have a small ribcage. It just wouldn't occur to me to do something like that. And also, if you could have your ribs removed, you'd have a scar and everyone's seen pretty much all of my body and you know, when you have work done – you can't remove a rib without leaving a scar. **1991**

If I wanted to have my face put on my back, it's my face, you know. It's like it's nobody's business what I do with myself. **1991**

My breasts drooped after my son Elijah was born, so I gave them a light lift and had a minor tummy tuck. That's all that's been done, I can assure you. Everything else is all mine. **1992**

The things I've had done, like my teeth and my nose, were really important to me. In movies my teeth looked really bad and I wanted to have them straightened. My nose was really big and I wanted it to be smaller. If that means I hate myself then I guess that's what it's going to have to mean. **1992**

I've always been pretty honest about it, you know, and it's strange because thinking if you were honest, people would go "alright" but being honest seems to have got me into an awful lot more trouble than I bargained for but, you know, people are going to talk about you no matter what it is that you do so I'm not so interested. I hate to say that I don't care what people think but I don't. **1992**

When I saw my face in *Mask* especially, I just thought I just want to get my teeth fixed, and my nose is huge. I don't want to see that close-up on that nose and those teeth anymore, so I went and had it done. I didn't loathe it, it just didn't work for me, you know. I didn't loathe my teeth... I mean, I had them all my life. I had them until I was 37 or something. I started getting them straightened then, and I had my nose the whole time, and it never bothered me. I thought it was kind of interesting. **1992**

Health And Fitness

I don't want women to think I'm full of shit. I don't want women to suddenly stop working out and say, "Fine, if only I had forty thousand dollars, I'd be in great shape!"

I started to work out because I started to have to dance and I didn't really know how to dance and then it makes me feel much calmer and really much nicer. **1991**

I work out – if I have enough time. I'll work out two, two and a half hours – I mean, that's if I have enough time. If I don't I'll come down and do an hour. And I never work on Sunday. I give myself time off and if I don't want to work on the weekend, I won't do it. I'm not – I don't think I'm fanatical, but it's a really big part of my life. **1991**

I exercise every day at home with weights and I swim. **1991**

I don't think it's a fad. I just think it's, I don't know how it works over here (UK), but in America it's just kind of 20 or 30 years old now, so I think it's past being a fad, and I know it works for me, it makes me feel better and look better and it's good for my mental health. **1992**

You don't get the best body you can have by wishing for it. You've got to work for it. You've got to sweat for it. **1992**

The biggest breakthrough I've made is to discover training techniques which halve the amount of time you need to spend in the gym. I realised my old demanding routines weren't working anymore so I found a new trainer and a new pattern. Because I had the courage to change my ideas. I'm seeing amazing progress with my body. **1992**

I don't see my body as a work of art, more a tool for my work. The stronger and more flexible I become, the better I can put myself across on stage and screen. **1992**

I don't have a perfect body, but in two months I'll be at my best. And in three months I'll look fabulous. **1992**

I work out for hours every day. There is not one piece of exercise equipment I don't know about. I practically kill myself for my body. **1992**

On Her Fitness Video

They came to me and asked if I wanted to do one. And I looked at a bunch of videos and I thought I could come up with something that would be better for me, that I would like because I couldn't find something exactly what I wanted when I went out looking at videos, so I made up a programme that was exactly what I would like to do, and it seems to be working really well. **1992**

Food

I drink a lot of water, but I don't like regular water. I like fizzy water, but that's good enough. **1991**

For keeping my weight the way I want to keep it, I don't like to eat really late. I like to eat my biggest meal early in the day and then have something light in the night, but I like to eat. I mean I can chow down and I really like to do it, but as I get older, I can see I have to make changes in the way I eat. **1991**

I tried a Big Mac, and I didn't like them, I must say. I just – I didn't like it. **1991**

I am not a complete vegetarian, but I don't really like meat. I like pasta and I like salads and I like souffles. I like things that are caloric, but we make them differently in the house. We really are conscious, you know. **1991**

I have to be interested in watching my weight now because I couldn't eat everything that I wanted to eat and be thin, so it's a trade-off for me now. **1991**

I'm not a chocolate fanatic. People ask me like what's a vice. And I don't drink, I don't smoke and I don't do drugs and chocolate is about as racy as I get. **1992**

I love chocolate and I like sweets a lot, I just have to be careful. **1992**

Me

I don't know what keeps me down to earth,
but it sure isn't ironing. I send mine out.

Even though I haven't been too crazy about some of the things I've done, I'm not ashamed of them either. I'm not ashamed of *The Sonny and Cher Show*. I don't think it's *Gone With The Wind*. Actually I don't think *Gone With The Wind* is *Gone With The Wind*, so let's just say it wasn't *Citizen Kane*. It's just not what I wanted to do.

I'm learning English at the moment. I can say "Big Ben", "Hello Rodney", "Tower Bridge" and "Loo". **1965**

Nobody tells me anything. Nobody dares to tell me anything. I want to be either successful or unsuccessful in reaching my goals or in whatever I do. It's like someone telling a painter, "I want you to paint a subject like this" or "Don't you use those colours". Then paint the fucking thing yourself and leave me alone! I want to do the work I want to do and if it's not successful then it's my decision or my fault or my choice.

I am literally terrified of flying. Once Sonny had to talk to me for three hours before I'd leave the airport. Now I get into the plane and take six sleeping pills and knock myself out for the whole trip. **1966**

We have a woman to cook and clean during the week. I don't really like the housewife bit. But at weekends she can't make it and I have to clean and cook lunch and make beds. It's what Sonny calls my womanly duties and he makes sure I do them. But heaven help anyone who comes in after I've cleaned up. They all have to take their shoes off before they come into the house. **1966**

I don't feel very rebellious any longer, maybe because I don't have to rebel against anybody now. But people seem to think I am, maybe because I, you know, dress strange and go out with young men. I think they give me a lot of qualities that I don't really possess because they want me to be so very different and rebellious. **1985**

The thing is you can ask me any question and I'll answer it. But none of it really matters to me... you'll never know me and the answer I give won't give you any real insight into me. You won't tap into my soul. **1985**

I really don't give a shit about what anybody thinks and all that stuff, I haven't for a lot of years. I just do what I want to do as the mood strikes me. **1985**

I still have a sixties mentality, I'm kind of rebellious. **1985**

I spent the first part of my life, I guess until I was 27, doing basically what other people wanted. **1990**

People ask me if I still have my ribs or how do I feel about my latest toy boy. I mean, come on. **1990**

Selfish? Absolutely true. I'm immature but I'm mature enough to realise it. Insecure? I'm insecure about everything. It doesn't take much to shake my confidence to the bone. I'm always mortified at things I say or do. **1990**

There was a picture on some magazine with me kissing another woman and the headline said I was leaving my boyfriend for her. They didn't say it was my sister. **1990**

I won't be the person people think I should be. I won't do what they think I should do. It was my mother's biggest problem with me too. It sounds really superficial, but the truth of the matter is we all want to do what we want to do. I'm not that ambitious – I just want to express myself. **1990**

I have the most opposite personalities that could possibly live in one body. Like, I'm obsessed with how I look, then sometimes I couldn't care less. I walk around the house like a bum. I'm concerned about my work, yet for two years I didn't work. **1990**

I've always taken risks, and never worried what the world might really think of me. **1990**

I've always been the kind of entertainer that stayed out in the public and yet magazines and tabloids and things and – are making it – me so much more reclusive where I don't want to go out. I don't really want to go out that much. **1990**

I certainly would like everyone to like me, but I also think that everyone's not going to be able to like me, you know, and also we make choices for the stupidest reasons, more so, I think, in America than other places that I've been, but I think it's a worldwide thing and so, you know, it's like we look at people and make some sort of a judgment. We want to know what they are. We don't want to have to think about it. We don't want to have to understand who they are. Like if you see a guy on a motorcycle with a tattoo, he's a Hell's Angel, all right. Well, you know what that is. I'm a lot of different things so you really have to think about... do you like what I'm doing, or if you don't like what I'm doing, can you still like me. If I get tattoos what else does it mean I do? You know, I mean – the tabloids have made a career out of thinking, "If she does that, well, she must just – she must do everything". **1990**

I'm really good to myself and I buy things that I want, but like I wanted a painting and it was just more money than I had ever spent for anything and so I just let it go. And I found something else that I think is really beautiful, not quite as beautiful, but I'll be real happy with it. You know, some things like I wouldn't scrimp on, but I don't know, I guess my tastes are good, but they're not outrageous. **1991**

It's like what I do is inside of me but how I present it, it comes in a package and if I want to continue to do like sing, do movies, I have to kind of keep up my body like it was any other piece of machinery or equipment. **1991**

I could answer your questions all day long. You guys are never going to know me or anything about me. So it's kind of a game. It's kind of a big pain in the ass. Personally I would just as soon watch or listen to what people do. I know you can't get to know people by interviews. It's my job to keep you as far away from who I am as possible. **1991**

I really don't think I have much of a temper. **1991**

Nice is kind of a boring thing and people say, "What's she like?" And they go "Oh, she's nice". Well, you know, there are lots of things that I'd like to be and nice just doesn't seem good enough. **1991**

I'm thoughtful. If someone needs something, I'm really great there. I will go to the end of the earth and I'm really helpful if someone's got a problem. I'm really willing to extend myself. **1991**

I'm not overly religious, I mean, not in any way that you could tell. **1991**

I've done so much more than I thought I would do, you know, and yet I'm not finished. There are things that I really want to do. **1991**

I think I'm cool. **1991**

When you have to go fight your battles and all the people you work with… I find myself now preferring to spend time with women when I want to fool around and have fun.

It's the women who don't get any applause who are really the heroines of my life because it's easy to do what I do.

I'm definitely my own person now. I'm the same person now, but I'm not that girl. **1992**

What's my perfect evening? – watching TV in front of a blazing fire, or chatting for hours with good friends like Meryl Streep, or Michelle Pfeiffer who's a real doll. Apart from these two, most of my friends knew me before I became famous. **1992**

You put something out there and you spend a lot of time trying to make an impression and once you've made it, then it's there. I've always tried to keep changing it so I never have to be stuck being something. I mean, I like acting and my heart's really in it when I do it but I'm not a serious actress. **1992**

I have a photographic mind, almost. I mean, if I read something slowly once, I can remember it almost in its entirety. Usually dyslexic people have some other sense or faculty that's very highly tuned to compensate. **1992**

I can't spell very well at all. And I have a hard time with the telephone sometimes. I invert numbers. I'm way too old to have it corrected or treated. I have a hard time with some concepts too. Like the only fight that Rob (Camilletti) and I ever got into was when he was trying to teach me how to do the 24 hour clock. I can't get the concept. I can't relate it to anything. Numbers and I have no real connection. I know them but our introduction was never really completed. **1992**

I'm prone to periods of unhappiness. I'm not an extrovert, I'm quite introverted and I can be really morose. Not for long periods but sporadically. **1992**

I'm vain. **1992**

It's not the business part of my business that I don't like. I like making films. I like being on stage. I don't like everything else that goes with it and every once in a while it gets to be too much and you just back away 'cause it's not like you can make a movie then go to Tahiti or something like that, there's lots of work. I could work constantly doing nothing. **1992**

I respond well to pressure. It's just that it built up for too long a period. I just needed to kind of let it go and just drop out of that phase of it and singing is easy – it's hard physically but there's no emotion. You don't have to do anything to stand up and sing, you just do it and nobody tells you what to do because you just do it, I mean it's not like being in a play. You're not someone else's idea of what's going on. **1992**

I like to go to the movies. I don't much like to go to concerts, but I like to go to movies a lot. I still like that. **1992**

I don't have that much free time. I'm working a lot on different things, you know, I've charities that I really am involved with and I just have things to do. **1992**

I do a lot of work for AIDS. I do a lot of work for Craniofacial Deformities in America. So I'm pretty involved with both those things. **1992**

I'm a woman's woman, I'm not really a man's woman, well, I guess I'm a man's woman, but I'm really a woman's woman. **1992**

I think women know that I really like them, and I mean I love men in a certain way but I really respect and like women. I like being with men and I think they're fabulous but I really prefer women. **1992**

I don't have any kind of problems with being honest. I really don't, because, you know, I'm a basically good person who does really stupid things, you know, and I've been mean, and I've been cruel and I've been you know, unthinking and unkind and I've been all those things, you know. **1992**

I've always been – I've been the same way since I was six years old and I was very frightening to my family because they just could never figure me out, you know, and I remember thinking that I was different from the time I was really little. I've never really changed that much. I'm always pretty much who I am. I'm very demanding, I expect a lot out of people that I work with. I give a lot I don't expect anyone to give nearly as much as I give, I don't expect anyone to work half as hard as I work so I expect a lot from everybody around me and I think it's also, I mean, for me to expect a lot out of someone is very flattering because I think they're capable and if they're not, I usually don't have too much to do with people who I don't think are very capable in some way or another. **1992**

I really like English humour. Dame Edna just rocks my socks. He makes me laugh so there's kind of nothing I can do about it, I do love comedy. I guess I have a real American taste but I like English humour too. It kills me. *A Fish Called Wanda* – I was totally mesmerised by it, and plus like the old Terry Thomas films. *Carry On Doctor* and *Carry On Nurse* – I've seen them, they're great films. **1992**

I cry every time I go to the English production of *Phantom Of The Opera* – it kills me. It's like my favourite time in a live theatre has been seeing that production. I've seen it a zillion times. **1992**

I get lonely. It's like now this is now going on for over a year that I haven't been with anyone and I would certainly rather be with someone than not, but I have great friends, I have a great family. I've had great, I mean, it's like my life is not a disaster without a man. My life is really a great life and it's more fun with someone to share it with when I'm not working but it's just really a fun life, you know. It's rough but I do fun things, I have fun people around me and so it's not that awful. **1992**

One part of you wants to tell what really happens, what really was the truth, who you really are and the other part of you kind of wants to keep a little like, something for yourself because the one thing that's kind of maddening, is that people think you're so many things that you really aren't, or do some of the things you don't do or whatever. I've always been very introverted as a person, very reclusive, but I find as the years go on I tend to be more so. **1992**

I don't have a problem with scripts. I can't call long distance, that is really trouble for me, numbers are really problems but I read very slowly but I have almost a photographic memory so once I read something I know it. I just have to read it very slowly. Dyslexia comes with like when I write, I don't spell well, because I'll start with the first two letters and go right to the last letter, it's a very strange thing. Like when I read signs I don't read, like on billboards I see things completely different than other people. **1992**

On Meeting The Queen

I was on my best behaviour and in my best dress. I was very ladylike and I curtsied, till hell wouldn't have me. I'd been practising in my room and then I saw her and I was very demure. I was completely covered from head to toe. It was black velvet and a long gown and it was great. **1991**

Being Tough

I just am so tired of having to defend all my actions and – when most of them – when what you hear is mostly not the truth anyway. It's just becoming like a big pain. **1990**

It's not bad for a poor girl who had to tie her shoes up with rubber bands. I'm determined never to let age or events stop me enjoying it for as long as I can. **1990**

I've always been a combination of very shy and very timid and very vulnerable and very very tough. It's like this guy – he's on CBS. He said, "You know, you're much different than I thought you were going to be. You're really nice and you're kind of quiet and you're really sweet", and I said, "Yeah, I am really". You know, he said, "You're so different than I thought you'd be and you're really sweet" and I – you know and he said, "I just can't – all the things I've heard about you and you don't seem like you could be anything but really gentle and sweet" and I said, "I'm really not. I'm very gentle. I'm really sweet, and if you fuck with me, I'd really mop the floor with you". **1990**

In my personal life I'm not very tough at all, but in my professional life, having to deal with being a woman in a man's world, I'm really tough. I never back down from a fight or an argument. I'm willing to stand there toe to toe with anyone. **1991**

I do have a really strong will and I am really disciplined. **1991**

I wouldn't give myself any advice, because advice is kinda bullshit. Take a deep breath and don't take any of it too seriously. **1991**

I think that, you know, maybe girls especially, were supposed to be nice, but being nice means do what people say to do and then I don't think you can really be nice. I'm a much nicer person now than before in my lifetime because I take care of myself first. **1991**

It wasn't that long ago actually that I was going to file for bankruptcy right before I shot *Witches*. There was about a two year period in there where things were kind of dicey. But, you know, you have to take – I mean sometimes those are the things that you get in life, you know. It didn't happen, thank God and so I'm sure it made me stronger or did something. **1991**

I wish I could talk to every kid and say, "Don't fuck with drugs, it's dumb". Telling them it's wrong is like telling them not to fuck because it's wrong – that has never worked.

Women have to harness their power – it's absolutely true. It's just learning not to take the first no. And if you can't go straight ahead, you go around the corner. That's what I would like women to get from me, nothing else.

I'm a perfectionist, my own boss. If someone isn't pulling their weight, I let them know. I'm a nice person but you can't say yes to everyone – I don't mean to sound so tough. I do get hurt and cry, that's the little girl in me. **1992**

I don't believe in advice too much. I believe in listening to advice and then doing exactly what you want to do. I'm very stubborn and manipulative and almost always get my way. This business is tough; people try to fuck with you every time you turn around. If you're a woman, I believe it's harder, because women aren't supposed to stand up for what they want. If you're nice, you'll get your arse walked all over, if you stand up for something, you're a bitch. There's no happy medium.

I'm sure there are lots of misconceptions that need to be addressed but that's not really my job to go around and explain myself. I put my work out there to be criticised. My private life is my private life and I don't care what people think about it. **1992**

Provocative

The truth is, I don't enjoy kissing people I don't know.

I just want to go out and have a good time. It doesn't mean I'm looking to fuck somebody. I just want to feel really sexy and appealing.

I have this sex-siren image, but really, I couldn't give a shit about that. I am so uninterested right now in all the Robert Redfords, Elvis Presleys and anyone else's husband that I really don't care. I feel it's almost like being a bank clerk. I go and do my job, and that's my job, the sex queen stuff. **1988**

My behind and stomach are very sexy and trim for a woman of my age. I won't let on what I don't like because everybody would focus on them. I read somewhere that one of my breasts is higher than the other. That's bull – they're beautifully balanced! **1992**

I see nothing wrong with posing nude at all as long as it's tasteful. But my stage costumes are so skimpy that there's little else for me to show. **1992**

I always wanted to be an animated character. And basically that's what I do now. I'm kind of an X-rated Cinderella. **1992**

I fall in love for about fourteen months and then afterwards, I love the person, but I just don't want to be with them anymore. I move on… when it starts to get too intense, I have to go… when it gets to be where you have to really make a commitment then I have to go.

I don't spend too much time thinking about nakedness. I looked at that picture of my backside and thought it was really beautiful. I didn't think it was a porno picture and I didn't think it was Venus De Milo, I just thought it was an interesting shape and that idea, Cher's Back, is really good. It's not literally selling my ass! I don't know is it? I guess it is in a way. It's a way of attracting people and using it to mesmerise. **1992**

I think that sex is great but I don't know that sex and nakedness have too much to do with each other. **1992**

Being naked or being lightly dressed is not a huge comment on my thought processes. I can go from being completely naked to going into *Silkwood* and having no make-up on, and being completely naked that way, but no-one comments on that. **1992**

Age

It frightens me that one day it's going to be... menopause! That I'm going to wake up and start being crabby and not want to go to Disneyland. **1990**

I used to worry about getting to 30, and then being 40, and now, at 44, I'm thinking these are the best years of my life. If this is old age, then honey, it really ain't all that bad. **1990**

I think that 40 was my favourite year, it was really a great year. So much happened and it was really – you know, on my 40th birthday, I got a call from the director of *Witches of Eastwick* and he said, "You know, I'm sorry, you can't play the part that you want to play because you're just not sexy enough and we want someone really – you know, these love scenes with Jack". And I'm sitting there and my children and my friend are bringing in a cake with a bellhop singing Happy Birthday and I'm sitting there with tears streaming down my face 'cause George Miller is telling me that I'm not young and sexy enough. And then, I met Robert and we had – you know, we had the best time. Actually, I met him the night before, but I didn't talk to him. And then I did *Moonstruck* and then I did *Suspect*. **1991**

I think I'll always look really good for what my age is, and that'll be fine. **1991**

At 70, I think I'd like to see myself far, far away from work. I'd like to be on an island some place, pottering around, gardening and sculpting and being completely away from civilisation. **1991**

I wish I could never, ever grow old. That's why I kill myself with exercises. **1992**

Fame And Fortune

We just do not know how to thank everyone concerned for making our name so big in so short a time. We are indeed honoured. Thank You. **1965**

Many others have had a much more difficult time giving up their privacy than I have, but it's something you don't know about at first.

I honestly think fame has to do with something that was lacking when you are small. Because all it is when you perform and people clap for

My life is not up for criticism, just my work. **1991**

I come from a very poor background so this will never be second nature for me. I appreciate it but I'm not like my children who just don't think about wealth. **1992**

I've never really been anything else but famous. I have a little bit of a hard time in crowds. **1992**

I believe there is always money to be got, and you just have to work for it. **1992**

Friends

I was at a party the night before the Oscars and *Silkwood*. Henry Kissinger walked in and he said "Cher!" I said "Hen!" And we hugged and talked. Val Kilmer said, "I've never really been impressed with anyone you've known but I'm impressed that you call Henry Kissinger, Hen!" I have a lot of friends people wouldn't necessarily connect me with! **1990**

Winona (Ryder) came up to me and said, "God Cher, something came out about me and it wasn't

you – it's that these people out there love you for the moment. Certainly, you're expressing yourself. But what you're getting back is well, it's just love.

I'm scared to death of being poor. It's like a fat girl who loses 500 pounds but is always fat inside. I grew up poor and will always feel poor inside. It's my pet paranoia. **1982**

I've been famous all my life and it's not as if I get upset if people notice me on the street. People say I've lived my life in public but that's only insofar as, when you go places, photographers take your picture and journalists put it down in their columns. After 20 years, it all piles up, so people have this fixed idea about me. **1985**

I've been famous since I was 18, it's part of my life and I don't mind it at all. **1985**

I want to be richer so I don't ever have to worry about money. I'm not afraid to work for it if I have to.

I am a trivia question. It's really shocking too, to pick out. **1990**

Cher with with Simon Le Bon of Duran Duran.

true" I looked at her and thought, "She's only 19". I mean, I started in when I was 18 and I've been able to outlast most of the people who wrote the stories. **1990**

I cry every time that terrible disease (AIDS) claims the life of someone close to me. I also get upset when I row with my mum as we often take a long time to make up. **1992**

Inner Thoughts

Everybody should really love one another, because nobody's here on earth for that long a time. **1965**

I just have the feeling that people can't cope with drugs. If they could, it would be a different story. But I don't know anyone who can handle them. Drugs handle people, not the other way round.

I don't drink and don't smoke – certainly don't do drugs. Not because I wouldn't if I wanted to – it's just not me – although one of my husbands was a heroin addict. One reason my friends are younger writers and directors is because the older ones tend to label me outrageous, what to me is everyday and natural. **1985**

I like my work, I love my work and I don't, I mean when I do my work, when I'm working on a specific thing, I'm very concentrated on it. I'm very serious about it, but I don't like the label a serious actress or serious singer. Just seems, you know, seems silly. I don't like labels very much to begin with and these two silly ones I don't need. **1992**

I was selling Cher when it wasn't so fashionable and acceptable to have a tattoo or a younger boyfriend. But... I just don't like the world around me very much. It's not a great place and I don't know if I'm adding anything to it. I need to figure out a way for me to do something that feels more honest or more worthwhile. Because entertaining doesn't seem that important to me when I see the stuff that's going on. And I don't know if its effect on me is enough to keep me doing it. **1992**

I'm going through a very strange and very agitating time in my life because if I was a young person I'd be an anarchist. A revolutionary, if I had more energy. Things are really fucked and I don't like what's going on. I'm not even sure how much longer I'm going to do this because I'm not sure where I fit or if I want to fit. I love performing but I don't know if I like being Cher anymore. **1992**

I don't know what else I would do although I know that whatever I do, I would do it well. I'm not sure where to put my energy. **1992**

Music and movies are like children. You can't ignore one while paying attention to the other, but you can't linger too long. **1992**

I was having a particularly hard time when I called my therapist. I said, "You don't know me. My name is Cher. I need a therapist. I need someone just like you. I think I'm having a breakdown. I live in Los Angeles. I need someone right away". It was a crisis for me, and I was dead serious, and I was dead into it and I hated it in the beginning. It was so difficult. My therapist is like my second mother. My therapist brought me up again, and she didn't say, "Everything was wrong, and you can't do this and you're not supposed to do this and you can't feel this". She taught me a whole bunch of feelings at one time, and nothing that you feel is wrong, and not to be critical of yourself and not to be critical of other people. I mean... I still talk to her. She moved back to Atlanta, but I talk to her once a week. She's the smartest person I know. **1992**

People are strange sometimes and they – if they had nothing happening in their life – then anything that happens in mine seems to be interesting. **1992**

I find myself feeling like I felt when I was a teenager all of a sudden, and very rebellious, and I am really angry about things, and I don't know what I want to be when I grow up. I hate the state of my country. I'm really pissed off, you know. I hate what's going on here. I hate the kind of chaos the government is causing. **1992**

I am the kind of Cher that I want to be. It's just that it's time for me to shift focus a little bit. I'm not exactly sure what that's gonna be, but I always feel like a change coming on.

Politics

I have a lot of ambitions about making the condition of our lives better but I don't think that government is really the place to do it because I think they're all really... can I say full of shit on English television? **1991**

Cher with Chastity and (right) Caroline Kennedy.

It seems the strangest people can become the heads of countries. **1992**

I'm way too honest to go into politics. **1992**

My history is far too liberal to go into politics. Because in America, we have a very hypocritical way of thinking. It's like, you know, if someone had had an affair, you wouldn't be able to be President and yet most of our Presidents have been, you know, whatever you call them. People don't tell the truth and people aren't interested in the truth, they're interested in someone who makes a good package. **1992**

Our Government (US) makes me cry, because they're such assholes. I'm really an American, and it's really hard for me to see people that I wouldn't let wash my car, making the decisions. **1991**

On The US Election 1992

It's kind of a totally bullshit kind of an affair. It's like, who has the best script writer and who does best on TV. **1992**

At Home

People ask why you need anything larger than twenty two rooms. You don't *need* any more than a living room, kitchen, bedroom and bathroom. But what you *want* is something else again. **1967**

Where I live right now is kind of – it's not the most trendy and it's not the least trendy. It's real nice though. **1990**

I can't really get attached to houses. I build and decorate and then sell them. I'm thinking of selling the Malibu home right away. Life is changing, and I'm getting all excited about what I'm going to be when I grow up. **1992**

I actually settled in one for ten years and then I sold it and since then I haven't really, I mean that was my home that was kind of my one and only home in my grown up life and now I feel I'm just kind of I'm floating. **1992**

I like to have two houses where everybody can be in one and I can just go in and out as I want to, 'cause I really like to have my own privacy, but I like to know that there is life happening out there if I want it. **1992**

The Things They Say About Cher

Two thousand years ago, Cher was one of the most powerful
queens of Ancient Egypt. She demanded total control and this
character trait has followed her down through the ages.
James Vaan Praagh (Cher's personal astrologer)

Don't believe any rumours about her. You shouldn't have any preconceived ideas about her. She's very, very open and sweet and girlie – like a teenager.
Winona Ryder (co-star in Mermaids)

I am such a big fan because there is nobody on the planet like her. **Oprah Winfrey**

I think she's got a great voice. **Jon Bon Jovi**

The way that Cher functions is quite extraordinary. There is absolutely no bullshit about her. She is incapable of self- censorship.
Eric Stoltz. Co-star: Mask

We think of her as the epitome of the American Woman. **Vogue Magazine**

Cher is probably one of the most sensitive people in show business. She feels. That's what's important. And she lets it out.
Sandy Dennis (co-star in Come Back To The Dime And Five, Jimmy Dean, Jimmy Dean)

I felt so intimidated at the very thought of meeting Cher. I mean, in photos she always looks so wonderfully thin, and so beautiful and stylish. The first thing that struck me when we did meet was how different she is in private life from the public image of her. Cher seemed, well, like anyone else. Very real. Very honest.
Meryl Streep (co-star in Silkwood)

Cher gets scared by herself. I don't know if she'd perform without me but she doesn't mind singing alone and of course our harmony is a big part of our songs. My voice isn't great on the solo parts but you don't notice it as much on the harmonising! **Sonny Bono**

My aunt is paying me $60 to get her tickets to see Cher. **Ken Dykes**

No one else has Cher's ease. And no one else has those armpits. Cher has the most beautiful armpits in the world. As much as anything else, I designed for her armpits.
Bob Mackie (Cher's designer)

Cher has something. I don't know what it is. Maybe it's the ability to make people feel. And to do that, maybe you have to experience a lot of pain, like Cher has.
Georgia Holt (Cher's mother)

Her timing is natural and almost infallible.
Norman Jewison (Director of Moonstruck)

Historically, Cher has been underrated. Look at the facts, of all the girl singers who saw chart action in the sixties, she, Diana Ross, Aretha Franklin, Dionne Warwick, and one or two others still have wide ranging careers. Where's Dusty Springfield, Lulu, Mary Wells, Marianne Faithfull, Ronnie Spector, Dee Dee Sharp, Nancy Sinatra, Bobbie Gentry and the rest of them? They're all in obscurity somewhere.
Rick Wilson (rock historian)

I never thought she was even going to be a singer. I thought she was going to be an actress or something, but never a singer.
Georgeanne (Cher's sister)

Cher's philosophy is if you've got it, flaunt it. And she's certainly got it.
Bob Hoskins (co-star in Mermaids)

The Things Cher Says About Them

Cher and Michael Jackson at the Los Angeles opening of the new show
"Dreamgirls" at the Shubert Theatre in Century City, 1983

Michael Jackson
He was a lot cuter before.

Madonna

I think she's unbelievably creative. I'm amazed at the amount, because in my day I was pretty good at doing the same thing that she's doing, but she does it so much better, but she's unbelievably creative, but she's not unbelievably talented. She's not beautiful and she's rude. But I really don't have anything against her, I do respect that she goes much farther than anyone should go, and I think that's interesting that she's willing to do whatever she wants to do.

The Rolling Stones

Look at the Rolling Stones, those guys are ancient. They're older than I am.

Meryl Streep

I'd still love to be Meryl. She really gets inside a part, lets the character wear her and take control. When I act, I still feel like it's really me.

Rusty Dennis

She is tough, but she has an edge of softness about her. She laughs a lot. She's soft spoken and very warm, with a metaphysical side to her about finding her way through life. She is also quite beautiful, even though when she speaks you hear those biker expressions.

Eric Clapton

He's very nice.

Eric Stoltz

I was one of the only people ever to see him without his make-up, and he and I became really good friends. He stayed at my house and we just spent a lot of our time together. So he was like two people to me.

Jane Fonda

I don't think I could be as strong as she has been to do what you believe in, even when it goes against everyone else's opinion.

Prince Charles

I'm fascinated by how much he knows about architecture. It's wonderful that he cares so passionately about protecting many of Britain's old buildings.

Bob Dylan

He was recording for David Geffen when I was living with David and we became friends. I always liked him because I recorded his songs from the beginning of my recording career. We all lived out on the beach at the same time and Sara and the kids and us spent holidays together and stuff. I like his sense of humour more than anything else.

Nicholas Cage

Nicky never plays it safe. You could play a role five different ways, and he'll go to the one where you've got the most to lose. He works alone, he acts alone and you kind of act alone with him.

Phil Spector

Philip was always strange. Always a very strange man. But he was really young at the time. I was 16 so he could have only been in his early twenties I guess. Sonny and Jack (Nitzsche) were 28 so Philip must have been maybe 22. I remember the first time I met Philip, he'd been taking French lessons and when we were first introduced he said to me, in French, "Will you go to bed with me?" And I said to him, in French "For money?". I was really taken aback that he would be that condescending. It pissed me off. So we had a very strange relationship from that moment on. But we always liked each other. I didn't always approve of his behaviour because he could be a real dick, really treacherous and a complete megalomaniac. But he was weird. He would fuck with the people he could and wouldn't with the people who wouldn't stand for it. He was like a child in that he'd push you to see what the boundaries were.

Robert Camilletti

My friendship with Robert is better than almost my friendship with anybody.

Elton John

He is one artist who truly transcends time. He's proof that this is the first time in history that parents and children can love the same music.

Bob Hoskins

I fell so in love with him in *Mona Lisa*, and I really wanted to work with him. He doesn't sound very American to me, but I didn't care, I just loved him.

Winona Ryder

I'd seen her in *Beetlejuice*. I thought she was so perfect, and she reminded me of myself when I was younger and I just thought she'd be great and we look like each other.

Robert Altman

I have to credit Robert with being fearless enough to hire me. He truly doesn't care about the outcome as society sees it when he works. He got me my start.

Jimmy Carter

He was too honest for the system.

Donovan

He's my favourite person, sweetest guy in the world. The thing about Donovan is that he believes.

The Walker Brothers

I used to know the Walker Brothers back home when they sang with their sister as their lead vocalist. Great guys.

Winona Ryder.